What's the Issue?

T0014543

WHAT'S A PANDEMIC?

By Simon Pierce

KidHaven
PUBLISHING

Published in 2023 by
KidHaven Publishing, an Imprint of Greenhaven Publishing, LLC
29 East 21st Street
New York, NY 10010

Designer: Andrea Davison-Bartolotta
Editor: Jennifer Lombardo

Photo credits: Cover (top) eldar nurkovic/Shutterstock.com; cover (bottom) Twinsterphoto/ Shutterstock.com; p. 5 (main) Ternavskaia Olga Alibec/Shutterstock.com; p. 5 (inset) Pee Paew/ Shutterstock.com; p. 6 Alexey Seafarer/Shutterstock.com; p. 7 Gorodenkoff/Shutterstock.com; p. 9 (globes) Ridackan/Shutterstock.com; p. 9 (background) Beautiful landscape/Shutterstock.com; p. 11 FamVeld/Shutterstock.com; p. 13 (top) Wikimedia Commons/File:1918_flu_in_Oakland.jpg; p. 13 (bottom) Wikimedia Commons/File: 1918_Spanish_Flu.png; p. 15 (top) Marco Rubino/ Shutterstock.com; p. 15 (bottom) stockelements/Shutterstock.com; p. 16 5D Media/Shutterstock.com; p. 17 Halfpoint/Shutterstock.com; p. 19 creativenv/Shutterstock.com; p. 21 Manuchi/ Shutterstock.com.

Cataloging-in-Publication Data

Names: Pierce, Simon.
Title: What's a pandemic? / Simon Pierce.
Description: New York : KidHaven Publishing, 2023. | Series: What's the issue? | Includes glossary and index.
Identifiers: ISBN 9781534542259 (pbk.) | ISBN 9781534542273 (library bound) | ISBN 9781534542266 (6 pack) | ISBN 9781534542280 (ebook)
Subjects: LCSH: Epidemics–Juvenile literature. | Communicable diseases–Epidemiology–Juvenile literature. | Communicable diseases–Prevention–Juvenile literature. | Public health–Juvenile literature.
Classification: LCC RA653.5 P54 2023 | DDC 614.4–dc23

Printed in the United States of America

Some of the images in this book illustrate individuals who are models. The depictions do not imply actual situations or events.

CPSIA compliance information: Batch #CSKH23: For further information contact Greenhaven Publishing LLC, New York, New York at 1-844-317-7404.

Please visit our website, www.greenhavenpublishing.com. For a free color catalog of all our high-quality books, call toll free 1-844-317-7404 or fax 1-844-317-7405.

Find us on

CONTENTS

Understanding Diseases

Many diseases, or sicknesses, are caused by pathogens. "Pathogen" is the scientific name for a germ. The most common pathogens are viruses and bacteria. However, **fungi** and **parasites** can also be pathogens. Many diseases that are caused by pathogens are contagious, meaning you can spread them from person to person by passing on the pathogen. A person who has a pathogen is said to be infected.

Some diseases aren't caused by pathogens, so they aren't contagious. For example, someone gets cancer when cells in a part of their body start **mutating**. They can't pass on the cancer because it's part of their body.

Ringworm is an example of a disease caused by a fungus.

ringworm fungus

Facing the Facts 🔍

Some diseases are less contagious than others. For example, malaria is a disease caused by a parasite that infects some mosquitoes. It can only be spread from one human to another through blood.

Words to Know

A disease that is constantly present to some extent in a certain place is said to be endemic. For example, the flu is endemic to the United States. You can catch it at any time of the year, although it's most common in the fall and winter. The word "endemic" is often confused with "epidemic," but they're different. An epidemic happens when a disease spreads faster than normal in a certain place.

An outbreak and an epidemic are the same thing, but an outbreak covers a smaller area. For example, if half your school gets the flu at one time, that's an outbreak. If half your state gets it, that's an epidemic.

6

Facing the Facts 🔍

"Endemic" can apply to things other than disease. For example, polar bears are endemic to the Arctic.

An endemic disease can still be **dangerous**. Between 2010 and 2020, more than 140,000 Americans had to go to the hospital because of the flu.

From Epidemic to Pandemic

Pandemics start out as outbreaks, then expand to epidemics. First, a few people in one area get a disease. They pass it on to more people, who pass it on to even more people. Travelers bring the disease back to their home country, where it spreads further.

An epidemic becomes a pandemic when it spreads to multiple countries. Remember that a disease can be endemic to more than one country, but it isn't a pandemic until more people than usual are all getting the disease at the same time. If someone brings a disease home with them but doesn't spread it to anyone else, it's neither endemic nor pandemic.

To remember the difference between an epidemic and a pandemic, remember that "pan" means "all" in Greek.

ENDEMIC

EPIDEMIC

PANDEMIC

Facing the Facts

Many scientists think COVID-19 (coronavirus disease 2019) will become endemic at some point in the future. Just like people can get a flu shot every year, they might also be able to get a COVID-19 shot every year.

9

Problems with Pandemics

Pandemics are dangerous for several reasons. First, many diseases can be deadly. If a person gets very sick, they might **recover** if they can be treated at home or at a hospital. However, with so many people catching a disease during a pandemic, hospitals fill up quickly. There might not be enough room for everyone who needs a bed.

Even during a pandemic, there are other reasons people might need to go to the hospital. When a hospital fills up with pandemic patients, people with broken arms or heart problems might need to wait hours to be seen by a doctor.

Facing the Facts 🔍

Doctors and nurses can get sick when they help contagious patients. They can also have problems with their **mental** health from working more than usual and watching so many people die during a pandemic.

The extra **burden** a pandemic puts on a country's hospitals is also very bad for the doctors and nurses who work in them.

Spanish Flu

In 1918, a flu virus started a pandemic. No one knows exactly where it started, but we know that it was brought to the United States by soldiers who were returning from World War I. This disease, which came to be called the Spanish flu, infected about one-third of the world's **population**. Overall, about 50 million people died because of this pandemic.

At that time, scientists didn't have any kind of medicine to fight the flu. People tried to avoid getting it and spreading it by staying away from each other, wearing face masks, and **disinfecting** surfaces.

Facing the Facts

In many countries, newspapers weren't allowed to print news about the pandemic because leaders didn't want to affect **morale** during the war. Spain was the only country where people could write about it, so readers thought it came from there.

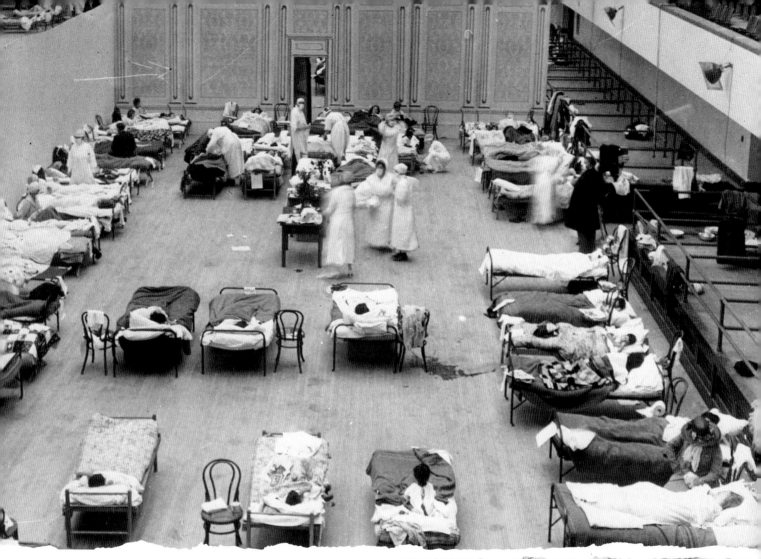

During the Spanish flu pandemic, hospitals were so crowded that doctors had to put sick people in other places, such as this auditorium. To stop the spread, people wore masks, including kids.

COVID-19

About 100 years later, a coronavirus started infecting people in China. Coronaviruses are a family of viruses. They've been around for hundreds of years, but this was a new kind. It caused the disease now called COVID-19, which became a pandemic. Hospitals filled up, and people started wearing masks and staying away from each other just like they did in 1918.

Thanks to advancements in medicine, scientists made several **vaccines** for COVID-19 in a little more than a year. People who get the vaccine are less likely to get the disease. Those who do still get sick are much less likely to need to go to the hospital.

Facing the Facts

Because the virus that causes COVID-19 kept spreading, it started mutating into a form that let it slip past the original, or first, vaccines. This is why many people need extra shots called boosters.

In 2020, many states told people to stay home to avoid spreading COVID-19. Because of this, places where there are normally a lot of people, such as Times Square in New York City, were empty.

How to Fight a Pandemic

To stop a pandemic, people need to stop the pathogen from spreading. This is hard, so we need to do more than one thing at a time. Wearing a mask and staying about 6 feet (1.8 m) away from other people if possible makes it harder for some pathogens to jump from one person to another. Washing your hands and disinfecting surfaces also stops pathogens from being spread by touching things.

If only a few people do these things, the pathogen will continue to spread, and the pandemic will get worse. This is why it's important for everyone to work together and practice good **hygiene**.

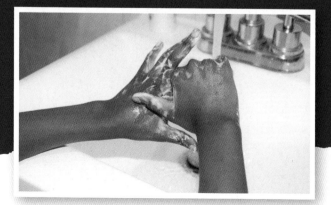

Facing the Facts 🔍

Isolating means staying away from others the whole time you're sick. Anyone who finds out they have COVID-19 should isolate themselves because masks and social distancing aren't foolproof.

Germs can spread when people touch their face and then touch someone else's hand. Since you don't touch your face with your elbow, touching elbows became popular at the start of the COVID-19 pandemic.

Lies and Misinformation

Some people have spread false information since the beginning of the COVID-19 pandemic. Some say masks don't help stop the spread of disease. It's easy to see that this isn't true. If you cover your mouth and nose with your arm and sneeze without a mask, your arm gets wet. If you have a mask on, it doesn't.

Some people don't even think COVID-19 is real. They think that news reporters are making it up to scare people. This is also untrue. As of March 2022, 6.07 million people around the world have died from this disease.

Facing the Facts 🔍

Some people believe in conspiracy theories about COVID-19. This means they believe in fake stories, such as ones that say there's a secret group that caused the pandemic. People generally get tricked by conspiracy theories when they're scared and feel like something is out of their control.

FACT OR FAKE?

Fake	Fact
Masks don't stop disease from spreading.	Masks stop big droplets with pathogens in them from entering the air. Small droplets might still get through, which is why we combine masks with social distancing.
Masks make it hard to breathe.	At the 2022 Winter Olympics, the Canadian women's hockey team played an entire game wearing masks and had no problems breathing.
Vaccines don't work.	The COVID-19 vaccines have been proven to stop most serious cases of the disease.
Vaccines are dangerous.	In most people, vaccines don't cause serious problems. Getting the disease is much more dangerous than getting the vaccine.
COVID-19 doesn't affect kids.	Anyone can get COVID-19, and even if someone doesn't get very sick, they can make someone else sick by spreading the virus.
COVID-19 isn't real or dangerous.	Millions of people have died from COVID-19, and millions more have **permanent** lung and heart problems even after they recover.

Misinformation about COVID-19 can spread as quickly as the disease itself.

Actions to Take

To stop a pandemic, we need to work together, so everyone's actions matter. You can help keep yourself and others safe and healthy by wearing a mask, staying away from others if you feel sick, and social distancing. You can also point out misinformation when you see or hear it. Knowing the truth helps people make good choices.

Because of how many people travel every day, scientists say it's possible we'll have more pandemics in the future. Travelers can take a disease home before they even know they're sick. That's why it's important to know how to deal with a pandemic.

Facing the Facts 🔍

A lot of pandemics start with zoonotic pathogens, which means they come from animals. As humans keep destroying animals' **habitats**, these animals have to move closer to where people live, which makes it more likely that they'll pass a disease to humans.

WHAT CAN YOU DO?

Regularly wash your hands with soap and warm water for 20 seconds.

Wear a mask when you're around other people.

Follow social distancing rules when you can.

Speak up when you hear misinformation.

Learn more about pathogens and disease so you can spot misinformation.

Listen to scientists and doctors, not social media.

A pandemic is a scary time because it feels like a lot of things are out of our control. However, there are some actions everyone can take.

GLOSSARY

burden: Something that is hard to endure.

dangerous: Unsafe.

disinfect: To clean something in a way that kills all pathogens.

fungus: Any member of the kingdom of living things (such as mushrooms and molds) that have no chlorophyll and must live in or on plants, animals, or decaying material. The plural is fungi.

habitat: The natural home for plants, animals, and other living things.

hygiene: The things that you do to keep yourself and your surroundings clean in order to maintain good health.

mental: Of or relating to the mind.

morale: Feelings of enthusiasm and hope in an individual or group.

mutate: To change into something very different.

parasite: Living things that live in, on, or with another living thing and often harm it.

permanent: Lasting for a very long time or forever.

population: The number of people that live in an area.

recover: To get back to the way things were before.

vaccine: A medicine that keeps a person safe from illness.

FOR MORE INFORMATION

WEBSITES

BrainPOP: Coronavirus

www.brainpop.com/health/diseasesinjuriesandconditions/coronavirus

Learn more about COVID-19 with movies, quizzes, and games.

Kiddle: Pandemic Facts for Kids

kids.kiddle.co/Pandemic

Read more about what a pandemic is.

BOOKS

Bender, Marie. *Invisible Invasion: The COVID-19 Pandemic Begins.* Minneapolis, MN: Checkerboard Library, 2021.

Laughlin, Kara. *What Is a Pandemic?* Mankato, MN: The Child's World, 2021.

INDEX